The BROWN BOY WHO Made Me a MOM

I AM WHOLE

By Cadiesha Mckenly Wilford

Illustrated By Javaria Ali

To my J3, the amazing brown boy who made me a mom. I love you forever and always. And to all the brown boys who have changed our worlds for the better, by making us mothers, we cannot wait to see you make the world yours!

Oh, my precious brown baby boy.
Your arrival has brought me so much joy.

I am forever amazed by how peaceful you are. You have exceeded my every expectation, by far.

Watching you, waking or sleeping, brings me serenity. I still can't believe you are now part of my identity.

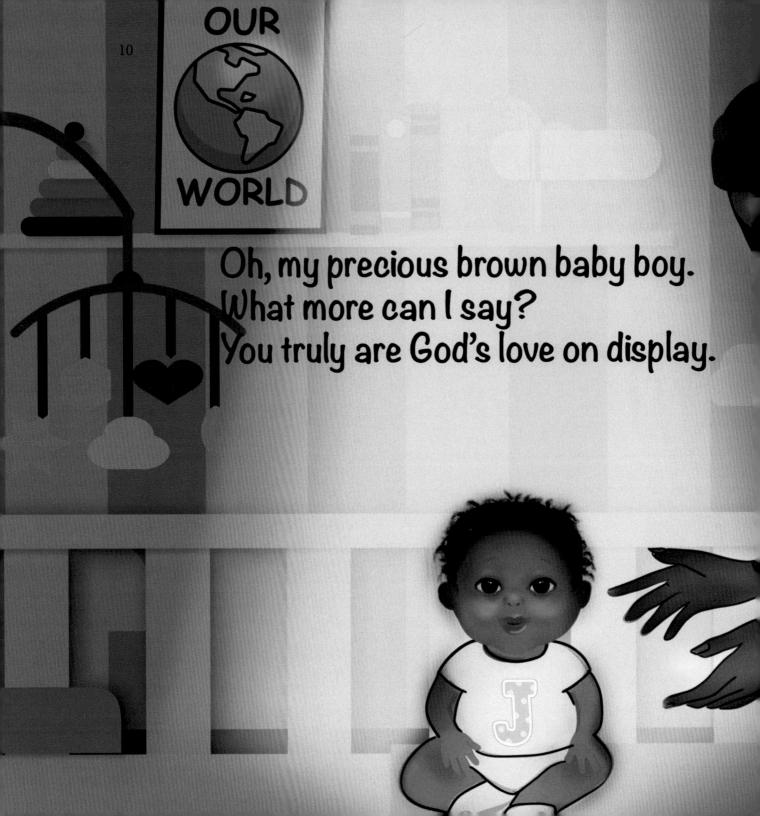

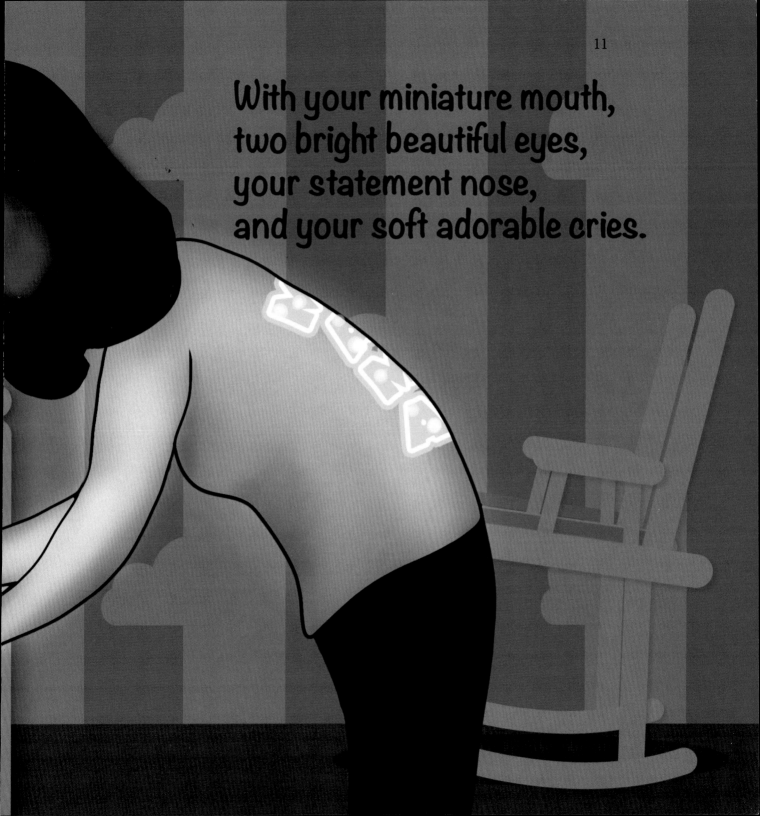

With your miniature mouth,
two bright beautiful eyes,
your statement nose,
and your soft adorable cries.

To think you grew with me from only an inner swirl. Your warm, innocent smile truly colors my world.

Your tiny little toes like little corn rows.
Eyes always curious, your excitement shows.

Strong hands hold tight to my finger.
The love in my heart will forever linger.

Oh, my precious brown baby boy.
Always remember that you are whole.
Strong, brave, and able to meet any goal.

Nothing can stop a beautiful soul like you.
Whatever you believe, that, you can do!

One day, you will make a big splash.
So many obstacles you will smash!

Until then, I promise to nurture your heart, expand your mind, and encourage your art.

Oh, the light you will bring to all you adore.
I can't wait to see you sing, to see you soar.

Not by what you have done,
but by simply being you, my son.